If you enjoy this book...

...look out, also, for the other wonderful Hanadeka cat and dog books which Helen Exley Giftbooks publish:

Utterly gorgeous cats (the companion volume to this book)
Utterly adorable cats
Utterly lovable dogs

Watch out, as well, for the _tiny_ books **Cats** and **Dogs** called *Jewels*, which have an amazing 368 pages, but fit snugly in the palm of your hand! You will also find the images in this book on a whole array of fluffy cats, fridge magnets, cat bowls, calendars, mugs, notebooks and giftbooks which we are distributing in a special spinner.

See what else we publish...

If you like this book, you should also visit Helen Exley's website to see the other giftbooks she publishes – everything from pet books to gifts for mothers, sisters and other members of the family, and books on timeless wisdom. Over 300 intriguing gift ideas are listed on the site:
www.helenexleygiftbooks.com

Published simultaneously in 2006 by Helen Exley Giftbooks in Great Britain and Helen Exley Giftbooks LLC in the United States.

Selection and arrangement copyright © Helen Exley 2006.
Copyright © Yoneo Morita 2006,
Licensed by Intercontinental Licensing.
The moral right of the author has been asserted.
ISBN 10:1-84634-147-7 ISBN 13: 978-1-84634-147-2

A copy of the CIP data is available from the British Library on request. No part of this publication may be reproduced or transmitted in any form or by any means, electronic or otherwise, without permission in writing from the publisher. Printed in China.

12 11 10 9 8 7 6 5 4 3 2 1

Helen Exley Giftbooks, 16 Chalk Hill, Watford, WD19 4BG,
Helen Exley Giftbooks LLC, 185 Main Street, Spencer MA 01562, USA.

Utterly wonderful
dogs

HELEN EXLEY

Whoever else thinks
you are of little worth –
to your dog you are
the heart
of his universe.

PAM BROWN, B.1928

A quiet, gentle dog
will bring a quiet,
deep satisfaction
to your whole life.

HELEN EXLEY

quiet and gentle

joy of living

"Whatever is, is good" – your gracious creed. You wear your joy of living like a crown.

DOROTHY PARKER (1893-1967)

He is born our friend;

while his eyes are still closed,

already he believes in us:

even before his birth,

he has given himself

to man.

COUNT MAURICE
MAETERLINCK
(1862-1949)

The average dog has one request to all humankind. Love me.

HELEN EXLEY

A man's best friend

is his dog. LORD BYRON (1788-1824)

To your dog, you are
more than just a friend;
you are the leader of the pack,
his protector, his provider,
and an all-knowing god.

STUART & LINDA MACFARLANE

...once a dog loves you,
it loves you always,
no matter what you do,
no matter what happens,
no matter how much
time goes by.

JEFFREY MASSON

loves you

Happiness is a warm

puppy

CHARLES M. SCHULZ (1922-2000)

my little

My little old dog:
A heartbeat
at my feet.

EDITH WHARTON (1862-1937)

dog

Dogs bring out the best in humankind.

PAMELA DUGDALE

the only love

Sign on bulletin board:
"Puppies for sale:
The only love
that money can buy."

money can buy

...I felt a silent current of love
from him – strong, steady and deep....
For someone who has never
had this kind of experience...
there are no words to adequately
explain it.

SUSAN RACE

Rarely did he take his beautiful,
kind eyes off me...
and wherever I went there he would be too,
and wherever I sat he would...
sit beside me – close, protecting me,
his head on my knee.

ELIZABETH VON ARNIM (1866-1941),
FROM "ALL THE DOGS OF MY LIFE"

loveliness

To hold a living creature, to learn its loveliness,
to feel its heart beat in our hands,
to know its trust, is at last to understand
that we are kin. Is to rejoice in life.
Is to lose all loneliness.

PAM BROWN, B.1928

Dogs, no matter
their breed, all have
an inner beauty.
They have
kind, gentle hearts
and a real need
for company
and affection.

STUART & LINDA MACFARLANE

happy

P eople need a measure
of happy simplicity –
   and a dog supplies it.
Unqualified love
   – and very
      few demands.

CHARLOTTE GRAY, B.1937

simplicity

C O

A life, a warmth,
an intelligence.
A kind companion.
A dog.

PAM BROWN, B.1928

mpanion

How can any of us

explain how we feel...

in the early morning,

when the animal we have chosen

to share our lives is standing...

waiting... to renew the pleasure

of our presence.

JOYCE STRANGER

Soft big eyes,

gentle and quiet.

She is patient and loving

– just what any

stressed-out

human needs.

HELEN EXLEY

believes

in you

A dog believes
you are what you
think you are.

JANE SWAN, B.1943

He will kiss the hand that has no food to offer.... He guards the sleep of his pauper master as if he were a prince.

SENATOR GEORGE VEST (1830-1904)

so sad

Every dog deserves

a smile, a word of admiration,

a little reassurance

– especially if he is very ugly

or very sad.

PAM BROWN, B.1928

fuzzy fur

Dogs are
effervescent,
fuzzy marvels
of nature.

MARI GAYATRI STEIN

Dogs come in
all shapes and sizes,
Yet every one,
you must agree,
Make humans
perfect company.

STUART & LINDA MACFARLANE

perfect company

D_{og, *n.*}

A kind of additional

or subsidiary Deity designed

to catch the overflow

and surplus of the world's worship.

AMBROSE BIERCE (1842-C.1914)

Heaven goes by favor. If it went by merit,
you would stay out and your dog would go in!

MARK TWAIN (1835-1910)

A dog knows that if he sits in front of you long enough and pleads with every look and wag – you'll eventually give in and take him for a walk.

PAM BROWN, B.1928

pleading

Puppies look like very small children
whose mothers have bought a size or two
too big clothes. To give them growing room.

MAYA V. PATEL, B.1943

baggy

p u p p i e s

...adorable little puppy

who will snuggle up

to you, nibble your ear,

gambol and romp

all over the place...

worming its way

into your heart,

making a slave of you....

BUSTER LLOYD-JONES

What can we call them!;
A huddle of pups?
A wriggle of pups?
A squirm, a shove
A muddle of pups?
A drowse of pups.
A sprawl of pups.
A totally out of this world of pups.
And all gathering the energy
to become a rush, a plunge,
a stampede of pups.

CLARA ORTEGA, B. 1955

They have a new puppy next door. I heard him singing in the night – a most mournful song of loss – mother and siblings, remembered smells and familiar faces.

No matter that his new bed is soft, that the light has been left on, that food and water is within reach. It is all too strange, too large, too lonely. He tries his range of voices – pleading, whimpering, howling – but no one comes. He is lost forever in a huge and unfeeling universe.

A week later and I meet him. The house is his. Bed, blanket, food dish, people. He greets me as a friend. All the world loves him – he is content.

CHARLOTTE GRAY, B.1937

Your little dog

has never even seen a rabbit –

but watch when he's asleep.

He's chasing down

a mammoth.

PAM BROWN, B.1928

little hunter

The smart dog
quickly discovers that,
to get what he wants,
one mournful look
is much more effective
than a frenzy of barking.

STUART & LINDA MACFARLANE

All right, so I don't know how to bury my garden messes. And I bark at everything. And I'm not very good at washing myself. And I roll in doubtful substances. And I smell a bit iffy in warm weather.

But I love you, love you, love you, and I will go on loving you till the day I die....

PAM BROWN, B.1928

What jolly chaps they are!

They are much superior

to human beings as companions.

They do not quarrel or argue with you.

They never talk about themselves,

but listen to you

while you talk about yourself.

JEROME K. JEROME (1859-1927)

A dog likes to sit
under the dining table.
Just in case.

PAM BROWN, B.1928

We believe in ourselves because of the trust our puppy has in us.

MARGOT THOMSON

He is your friend, your partner, your defender, your dog. You are his life, his love, his leader. He will be yours, faithful and true, to the last beat of his heart.

AUTHOR UNKNOWN

A wise dog

can teach us much

of what we need to know.

Patience.

Caring.

Companionship.

And Love.

PAM BROWN, B.1928

Most of us suffer from too much tension

and stress in the hustle of modern urban living,

where minute-by-minute considerations are

frequently complex and demand a whole range

of conflicting compromises. By contrast, the friendly

contact of a pet dog or cat serves to remind us

of the survival of simple, direct innocence even

inside the dizzy whirlpool we refer to as civilization.

DESMOND MORRIS, B.1928, FROM "DOGWATCHING"

How strange to think
Dog was once simply Dog.
For see how we have squashed him and stretched him.
Yet inside every variation
is that first and utterly basic Dog.

PAMELA DUGDALE

Every dog
is beautiful
in its own way.

STUART & LINDA MACFARLANE

T R

UST

A DOG WILL CONTINUE TO TRUST
WHEN IT HAS BEEN BETRAYED.

CHARLOTTE GRAY, B.1937

So my good old pal,
my irregular dog,
my flea-bitten,
stub-tailed friend,
Has become a part
of my very heart,
to be cherished till
life-time's end.

W. DAYTON WEDGEFARTH

Here's love.

Disguised as a mop.

PETER GRAY, B.1928

${\rm M}$ontmorency's ambition in life
is to get in the way and be sworn at.
If he can squirm in anywhere
where he particularly is not wanted...
he feels his day has not been wasted.

JEROME K. JEROME
(1859-1927)

BONES
BONES
BONES

I f a dog's prayers were answered,
bones would fall from the sky.

PROVERB

He toils not, neither does he spin, yet Solomon in all his glory never lay upon a door-mat all day long, sun-soaked and fly-fed and fat, while his master worked... to purchase an idle wag of the Solomonic tail, seasoned with a look of tolerant recognition.

AMBROSE BIERCE (1842-C. 1914)

the silent

s t a r e

...if he wanted a dog biscuit, he simply sat near the box
of biscuits and silently stared at one or the other of us.
If he not merely wanted a biscuit but felt
it was positively his right to have one, the silent
stare was accompanied by a lowering
of the head....

GEORGE PITCHER, FROM
"THE DOGS WHO CAME TO STAY"

Even asleep, he will detect someone

scraping out the last remnants

of Marmite from the jar in the kitchen

four floors below

and thunder downstairs to lick it clean.

TREVOR GROVE

Dog's maxim
on relaxation:
"The secret to being
completely relaxed is
to have a human to do
all the worrying for you."

STUART & LINDA MACFARLANE

One rattle of the biscuit tin

and you've got friends for life.

They sit and stare

with solemn eyes,

and if you don't take the hint,

you get barked at.

JANINE CHUBB, AGE 10

A dog's only ambition is to give you all his love.

STUART & LINDA MACFARLANE

love

The world
would be a sadder place
without puppies.

PAM BROWN, B.1928

puppies

Just a scruffy little dog....
And yet you are the best,
the kindest friend
anyone could have.

MARGOT THOMSON

At times it was like gazing into a human soul,
to look into his eyes; and what I saw there frightened me.
I tell you I sensed something big in that brute's eyes;
there was a message there, but I wasn't big enough myself
to catch it... it gave me a feeling of kinship all the same.
Oh, no, not sentimental kinship. It was, rather,
a kinship of equality.

JACK LONDON (1876-1916)

KINSHI

P

Happy is the dog

who has found a kind human

– he will forever have

someone to tickle his tummy.

STUART & LINDA MACFARLANE

'Tis sweet to hear

the watch-dog's honest bark

Bay deep-mouth'd welcome

as we draw near home;

'Tis sweet to know

there is an eye will mark

Our coming,

and look brighter

when we come.

LORD BYRON (1788–1824)

Poor dog! He was faithful and kind to be sure,

And he constantly loved me although I was poor;

When the sour-looking folk sent me heartless away,

I had always a friend in my poor dog Tray.

THOMAS CAMPBELL (1763-1854)

Your dog just doesn't notice that you
are old or ill or unsuccessful.

To him you are perfect.

PAM BROWN, B.1928

While I run my toes over his arched spine, I actually feel my tension easing and my bunched up muscles relaxing. I imagine (as most dog owners invariably do) that he "understands" me, understands what I'm saying to him.

SHOBHA DÉ, FROM "SPEEDPOST"

relaxing

...we simply loved them
with all our hearts;
we perhaps even loved them –
I'm not ashamed to say –
beyond all reason.
And they loved us, too, completely,
no holds barred.
Such love is perhaps the best thing
life has to offer.

GEORGE PITCHER,
FROM "THE DOGS WHO CAME TO STAY"

I have found

that when you are deeply troubled

there are things you get

from the silent devoted companionship

of a dog

that you can get

from no other source.

DORIS DAY, B.1924

Keesha was my friend,

my confidant, my angel

and, ultimately, my teacher.

SUSAN CHERNAK MCELROY

confidant,
angel, teacher

The rich man's guardian
and the poor man's friend,
The only creature
faithful
to the end.

AUTHOR UNKNOWN

faithfu

your

He is going to stick to you,

to comfort you,

guard you, and give his life

for you, if need be....

You are his pal.

JEROME K. JEROME (1859-1927)

pal

ABOUT THE AUTHORS

Yoneo Morita, who took the stunning photographs in the book, was born in Ito, Japan in 1950. He graduated in photography in Tokyo, and after working in a photographic library, has spent more than a decade capturing thousands of people's pets on camera. He adores dogs (he and his wife have twenty cats and six dogs in their own home), and has the patience – sometimes taking a week or more – to gain the friendship and acceptance of all his "models". This enables him to get the humorous, trusting and intimate "fish-eye" shots that have become his trademark. Yoneo Morita's work, with its familiar Hanadeka ("big nose") emblem, is now licensed to publishers and manufacturers in more than twenty countries around the world.

Helen Exley has edited and published several hundred books using her unique collection of quotations. Her books have appeared in more than fifty languages and are exported to over seventy five countries. Helen Exley personally chose all the quotations to match Yoneo Morita's photographs in this volume, and hugely admires his work. "I work with writers, illustrators and photographers across the world, and I regard Yoneo Morita as the top dog photographer of his time. He is a master of his art, and the results are just enchanting."

What is a Helen Exley Giftbook?

Helen Exley Giftbooks cover the most powerful of all human relationships: the bonds within families, and between friends, and the theme of personal values. Helen Exley's dogs, cats and many joke titles are fun, alternative gifts. There's a thoughtful book for all people, for all special occasions.
No expense is spared in making sure that each book is as meaningful a gift as it is possible to create: good to give, good to receive.
You have the result in your hands.
If you have loved it tell others.

Acknowledgements:
J.R. ACKERLEY: Used by permission of David Higham Associates. BUSTER LLOYD-JONES: from *Love on a Lead* by Buster Lloyd-Jones. Published by Secker & Warburg. Used by permission of the Random House Group Inc. JEFFREY MASSON: From *Dogs Never Lie About Love* by Jeffrey Masson, published by Jonathon Cape and Crown. Reprinted by permission of The Random House Group Ltd. DOROTHY PARKER: Extract from *Verse for a Certain Dog*. The author wishes to thank the NAACP for authorizing the use of Dorothy Parker's work. GEORGE PITCHER: from *The Dogs who Came to Stay* by George Pitcher. Published by Weidenfeld & Nicolson, reprinted by permission. CHARLES M. SCHULZ: Used with permission from United Media. MARI GAYATRI STEIN: From the book *Unleashing Your Inner Dog*. Art and text © 2001 by Mari Gayatri Stein. Reprinted with permission of New World Library, Novato, CA. www.newworldlibrary.com. ELIZABETH VON ARMIN: From *All the Dogs of My Life*. Used with permission from Little, Brown Book Group. EDITH WHARTON: Reprinted by permission of the estate of Edith Wharton and the Watkins/Loomis Agency.
Important copyright notice: Pam Brown, Janine Chubb, Pamela Dugdale, Helen Exley, Charlotte Gray, Peter Gray, Stuart and Linda Macfarlane, Clara Ortega, Maya V. Patel, Jane Swan, Margot Thomson: are all © Helen Exley 2006. Permission is not usually granted for use of even short quotes.